EXPLORING SCIENCE

GENETICS

A LIVING BLUEPRINT

BY DARLENE R. STILLE

Content Adviser: Irwin Rubenstein, Ph.D.,
Professor Emeritus, University of Minnesota, St. Paul

Science Adviser: Terrence E. Young Jr., M.Ed., M.L.S.,
Jefferson Parish (Louisiana) Public School System

Reading Adviser: Susan Kesselring, M.A., Literacy Educator,
Rosemount-Apple Valley-Eagan (Minnesota) School District

 COMPASS POINT BOOKS · MINNEAPOLIS, MINNESOTA

Compass Point Books • 3109 West 50th Street, #115 • Minneapolis, MN 55410

Visit Compass Point Books on the Internet at *www.compasspointbooks.com*
or e-mail your request to *custserv@compasspointbooks.com*

Photographs ©: Corbis, cover; Aneal F. Vohra/Unicorn Stock Photos, 4, 34; OneBlueShoe, 5; Bio-
photo Associates/Photo Researchers, Inc., 8; David Wrobel/Visuals Unlimited, 10; Getty Images,
11; Dr. David M. Phillips/Visuals Unlimited, 12; Charles E. Schmidt/Unicorn Stock Photos, 14;
BananaStock, 19; Photodisc, 21; North Wind Picture Archives, 23; Natalie Fobes/Corbis, 25
(top); Robert Dowling/Corbis, 25 (bottom); Phil Schermeister/Corbis, 27; Time Life Pictures/
Mansell/Getty Images, 28; Topical Press Agency/Getty Images, 30; Phil A. Harrington/Peter
Arnold, Inc., 32; Gary Randall/Unicorn Stock Photos, 36; Lester V. Bergman/Corbis, 37; Nick
Cobbing/Peter Arnold, Inc., 39; USDA/ARS/Scott Bauer, 40; Jeff Greenberg/Unicorn Stock
Photos, 42; Robert Holmgren/Peter Arnold, Inc., 43; Bettmann/Corbis, 46.

Editor: Anthony Wacholtz
Designer/Page Production: The Design Lab
Photo Researcher: Marcie C. Spence
Illustrator: Eric Hoffmann

Art Director: Jaime Martens
Creative Director: Keith Griffin
Editorial Director: Carol Jones
Managing Editor: Catherine Neitge

Library of Congress Cataloging-in-Publication Data
Stille, Darlene R.
Genetics : a living blueprint / by Darlene R. Stille.
p. cm. – (Exploring science)
Includes bibliographical references and index.
ISBN 0-7565-1618-8 (hardcover)
1. Genetics–Juvenile literature. I. Title. II. Series: Exploring science
(Minneapolis, Minn.)
QH437.5.S75 2006
576.5–dc22   2005025062

ISBN 0-7565-1763-X (softcover)

About the Author

Darlene R. Stille is a science writer and author of more than 70
books for young people. When she was in high school, she fell in love
with science. While attending the University of Illinois, she discovered that she also loved writing. She was fortunate enough to find a
career as an editor and writer that allowed her to combine both of
her interests. Darlene Stille now lives and writes in Michigan.

TABLE OF CONTENTS

CHAPTER ONE

A Living Blueprint

SUPPOSE YOUR FAMILY wanted to build a new house. One day, trucks came and dropped off lumber, bricks, panes of glass, spools of wire, and sheets of drywall. All of these things are parts of a house, but what is the house supposed to look like? How would the parts fit together to make bedrooms, bathrooms, a kitchen, and a living room?

The first step in building a house is having a blueprint, or sketch, that shows how the inside and outside of the house will look.

The frame of a house cannot be constructed without a set of detailed blueprints.

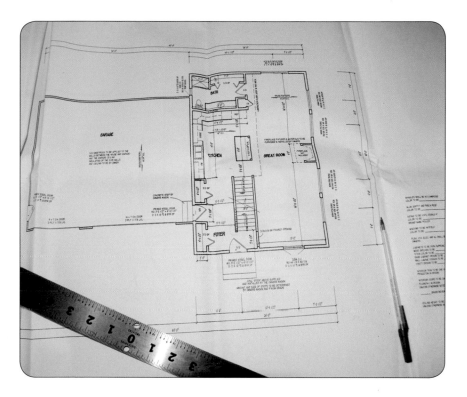

Your body and all other living things in the world also have a blueprint. This blueprint tells what an organism—any living thing—will look like, its chemical functions, and other vital information. For example, it determines whether hair will be curly or straight, whether the color of a flower will be pink or white, and whether or not the fur on a cat will be spotted. This living blueprint is made up of units called genes and is called the genome, which is the entire genetic makeup of an organism.

Every dimension and measurement is identified on a blueprint.

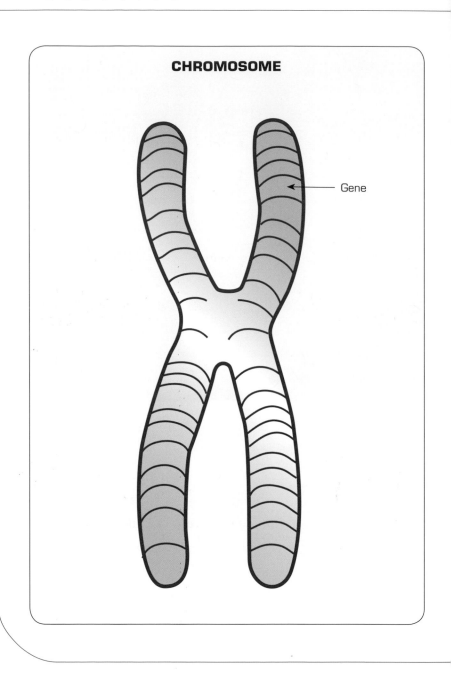

CHROMOSOME

Gene

Chromosomes contain about 25,000 genes.

WHERE GENES ARE FOUND

Animals, plants, fungi, and one-celled organisms are made up of cells. Threadlike structures called chromosomes are in a part of the cell called the nucleus. Genes are found within these chromosomes and are made of a chemical called deoxyribonucleic acid (DNA).

WHAT GENES DO

Each cell in an organism contains a complete set of that organism's genes. Genes carry a code, or set of instructions, that determine an organism's traits, or characteristics. Genes determine what an organism will look like and how it will function. However, not all of the genes are "turned on." Each part of the organism only uses the genes necessary for it to function. In a muscle cell, only the genes for muscle cells are turned on. In a plant leaf cell, only the genes for leaf cells are turned on.

Genes instruct the cell how to make proteins. Proteins build, regulate, and maintain your body. There are many different kinds of proteins. For instance, they build bones, enable muscles to move, control digestion, and keep your heart beating. Some proteins help repair and replace parts of the cell, and other proteins help with chemical reactions in cells. Because they identify the kind of protein for each cell, genes act as a

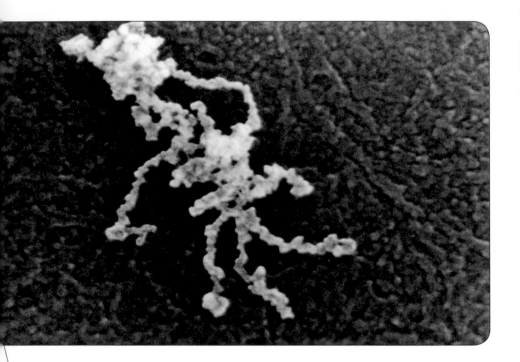

blueprint for an organism's growth and development. Each cell only makes the kind of protein that it needs to function.

WHERE GENES COME FROM

All organisms that reproduce sexually inherit their genes from their parents. In human beings and other animals, half of the genes come from the mother and half come from the father.

Chromosomes in human eggs and sperm determine whether offspring will be male or female. There are two sex chromosomes called X and Y. Eggs only carry an X chromo-

The traits you inherit from your parents are found in your genes.

DID YOU KNOW?

Different species have different numbers of chromosomes. Humans have 46 chromosomes in each cell, but cats have 38, and dogs have 78.

some. Sperm can carry either an X or a Y chromosome. Sperm and egg cells contain only 23 chromosomes each.

When the sperm and egg cells unite, the resulting fetus inherits half of its DNA recipe from its mother and half from its father. Two of these 46 chromosomes determine the sex of a person. A girl inherits two X chromosomes, one from her mother and one from her father. A boy inherits one X chromosome from his mother and a smaller Y chromosome from his father. Since genes code for all traits, some of a child's traits come from the mother and some come from the father.

The same is true for plants; during sexual reproduction, half of the traits passed on by genes come from a female plant part, and half come from a male plant part.

Even one-celled organisms, such as bacteria, that reproduce asexually inherit their traits through genes. A one-celled organism grows by dividing into two new organisms. The genes from the original organism are duplicated and passed on to the two new cells.

Clones

Some news stories about clones sound like they are straight out of science fiction. Has some scientist secretly cloned a human being? Will people one day clone themselves to create spare body parts? What is a clone, anyway?

Clones are simply two or more organisms that have the exact same genes. Clones are nothing new or unusual. There are many clones in nature. One-celled organisms, such as bacteria, create clones when they reproduce. The cell simply makes an identical copy of its genes and then divides in two.

Clones can grow from parts of some organisms. Sponges, for example, are marine animals that can reproduce asexually

by a process called budding. Small growths called buds appear on the sponge. The buds break off and become new sponges that are clones of the original sponge.

Plant clones are everywhere. If you put a piece of potato containing an "eye" in soil, a new potato plant with exactly the same genes will grow from it. There are even human clones in nature. Identical twins are clones because they share the same genetic

Although sponges can reproduce sexually, clones are only created through budding.

makeup. Identical twins come from one egg fertilized by one sperm. The fertilized egg, called a zygote, divides to form two identical embryos. These two embryos grow into identical twins.

Scientists can also create clones in the laboratory. They can clone individual cells and genes, and they can even clone entire animals. In 1996, they cloned the first mammal, a sheep named Dolly. In 2005, researchers cloned human embryos, which are the early stages of human development that form from zygotes. The researchers took individual cells from an embryo and made them grow into a new embryo with the same genes. This type of cloning is called artificial twinning.

Is it possible to clone a whole human being? No one is sure, but many people believe that it would be wrong to do. They also believe it is wrong to clone human embryos. However, some scientists believe that through the process of cloning, they will be able to cure diseases that were once incurable, such as Parkinson's disease. Unfortunately, there are many questions about cloning mammals that scientists cannot yet answer. For example, will the clone age faster than the original? Will the cloned animal be healthy?

Dolly died in 2003 from a progressive lung disease.

CHAPTER TWO

Heredity and Genes

HOW DO ANIMALS and plants pass genes to their off-spring? In sexual reproduction, new individuals come from the joining of male and female sex cells. The female sex cell is called an egg. The male sex cell is called a sperm. Eggs and sperm are different from the other cells that make up an organism—they have only half the

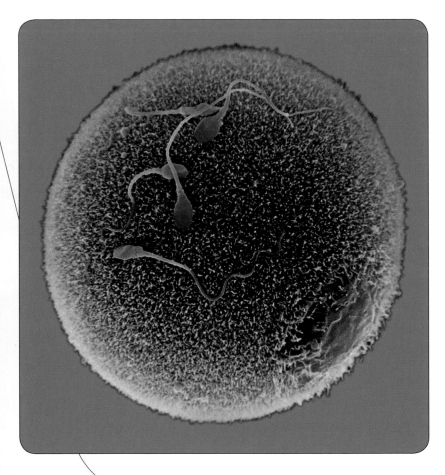

Sperm swarm an egg during sexual reproduction.

number of chromosomes compared to other cells.

Most of an organism's cells are body cells, which are also called somatic cells. Somatic cells have two sets of chromosomes. For example, a human somatic cell has 46 chromosomes grouped into 23 pairs. One set of 23 chromosomes in the pair comes from the father and one set of 23 comes from the mother.

Therefore, when the male sex cell unites with the female sex cell, each contributes half of the chromosomes. Because half of an offspring's genes come from each parent, the offspring receives a full set of 46 chromosomes.

DOMINANT AND RECESSIVE GENES

Genes for a given trait may occur in alternative forms that differ in their effects on the offspring. Alternate forms of the same gene are called gene alleles. For example, there is a gene that determines the color of your hair. That gene may have many alleles; for example, a gene allele could make your hair black, brown, auburn, red, or blond. You inherit one allele for each gene from your mother and one from your father. A gene can have two alleles that produce different effects. In pea plants, for example, there is a gene that affects plant height. One allele of that gene could code for tall plants, but another allele for the same gene could code for short plants.

Some alleles are dominant, while other alleles are recessive. The traits coded by dominant genes usually show up over those coded by recessive genes. Each of the two alleles you inherit for a gene may be strong (dominant) or weak (recessive). When an allele is dominant, it means that the

Traits in pea plants, as well as other living things, are different depending on the type of gene allele.

physical characteristic it codes for usually is evident in the living organism. You need only one dominant allele to express a dominant trait. You need two recessive alleles to show a recessive form of a trait.

WHAT ARE THE ODDS?

Children inherit traits from their parents according to the laws of probability. To understand the probability of inheriting a specific trait, one only needs to ask, "What are the odds?"

To calculate the odds, genetic scientists use a kind of shorthand for the alleles. They use capital letters to show dominant alleles and lowercase letters to show recessive alleles. An individual may have two dominant alleles, two recessive alleles, or one dominant and one recessive allele. The combination of alleles in an organism is called the genotype. The genotype's effect on how an individual looks or functions, in addition to environmental factors, is called the phenotype.

DID YOU KNOW?

Several genes working together determine many traits. Skin color, hair color, and eye color result from a combination of genes.

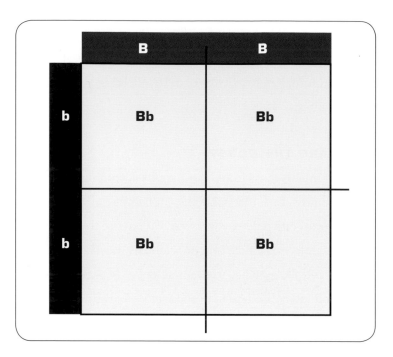

THE PUNNETT SQUARE

Genetic scientists use a device called a Punnett square. A Punnett square looks like a window divided into four panes. Along the top are the mother's genes. Suppose they are both dominant traits. If the trait is black hair, for example, they can be shown as BB. Along the side are letters representing the father's genes for hair color. Let's say that they are recessive genes for blond hair, which are shown as bb. In each square, scientists match up the two traits, as they would come together in real life. In this case, they would always create pairs of Bb alleles in the offspring. Since B is dominant, all the children would have black hair.

What if each parent has one dominant gene for black hair and one recessive gene for blond hair? The layout in the Punnett square shows that the dominant gene would be present in three out of four cases. That means there is a 75 percent chance that the offspring would have black hair. On the other hand, the offspring would only have a 25 percent chance of having blond hair.

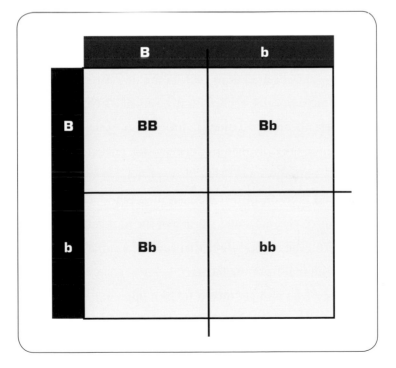

WHY EVERYONE IS DIFFERENT

You have probably noticed that family members usually resemble each other. However, brothers and sisters also look different from one another, unless they are identical twins. None of the children look exactly like either parent. We all have our own special look because of genetic variation, or differences among genes. These differences occur because of several factors that mix up genes.

Gene alleles get mixed up when male and female sex cells are formed. This special type of cell division is called meiosis. During meiosis, the sex cell's chromosomes replicate once. Because the cell then divides twice, the number of chromosomes in sex cells are cut in half. In the first division, the cell divides into two cells, each with two sets of 23 chromosomes. In the second division, the 23 chromosome pairs split apart, and the four sex cells that are formed each have one complete set of 23 chromosomes. This process, which occurs during the second division of meiosis, is called random assortment. The set of 23 chromosomes in each of the four cells contains a mixture of gene alleles—half that came from that individual's mother and half from the father.

Gene alleles also get mixed up by a process called crossing over, which occurs during the first division of meiosis. Sometimes a group of genes on one chromosome will change places

with another group on its paired chromosome. This switch can happen because the chromosomes line up very close together just before the sex cells first divide. Sometimes, these paired chromosomes break. When they come back together, groups of genes may have swapped places on the paired chromosomes.

Members of a family will often look alike, but they will also have features that set them apart.

CROSSING OVER DURING MEIOSIS

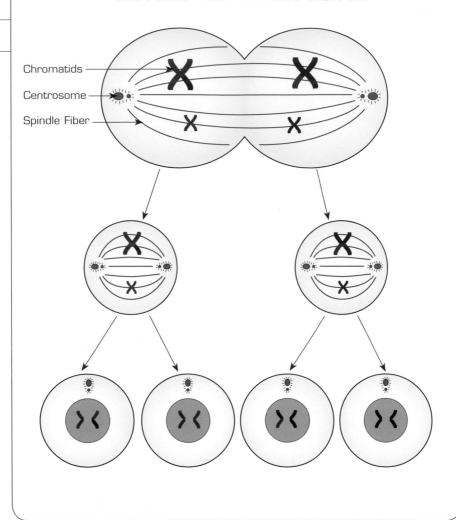

Genes also get mixed up when they pass from one generation to another. Your mother inherited her genes from her mother and father. Your father inherited his genes from his mother and father. Through mothers and fathers, the genes of grandparents are passed on to grandchildren. The grandchildren pass the genes along to other generations in the future.

Unimaginable Odds

In each egg and each sperm, there are millions of possible combinations of genes. That means that there are trillions of combinations that could result! This mix-up of genes creates an individual with genes in an order that has never occurred before and will never occur again. With the exception of identical twins, no two people are ever alike. To put it into perspective, a person in the United States has approximately a 1 in 700,000 chance of being struck by lightning in any given year. That means you would have a better chance of being struck by lightning millions of times in one year than guessing an exact combination of genes!

The chance of being struck by lightning is much greater than randomly picking a specific gene sequence.

CHAPTER THREE

Breeding Plants and Animals

ABOUT 10,000 YEARS AGO, people learned they could plant seeds from wild plants and grow those plants for food, year after year. They also learned how to tame some wild animals. Once they learned how to grow crops and gather animals into herds, they could spend some of their time improving how they lived.

BREEDING BETTER PLANTS

Over time, farmers learned that they could make better crop plants by breeding plants with good traits. For example, they only planted seeds from plants that produced the most food or tasted better. This kind of breeding is called selection. Eventually, the poor-performing plants died out, leaving only plants that were good performers. Without realizing it, farmers thousands of years ago had begun altering the genetic makeup of crop plants.

Breeding by selection was a slow process. Farmers had to wait for an improvement in a plant caused by a natural change in a plant gene. A change in a gene is called a mutation. A mutation, for example, could result in larger or juicier fruit on a tree. Then farmers only planted seeds that produced the better fruit. Even then, negative side effects, such as unhealthy or foul-tasting fruit, could result. The farmers had to weigh the benefits of the altered fruit with the possible consequences.

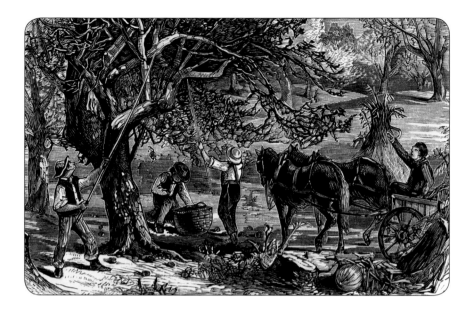

HYBRIDIZATION

Farmers took genetic alteration one step further when they began to cross different male and female plants in the late 1700s. The new plants that were created are called hybrids. To make a hybrid, a breeder selects two plants that have desirable traits.

For example, one kind of tomato plant might naturally have developed genes that cause it to produce large tomatoes. Another kind of tomato plant might have genes that prevent it from being harmed by a certain plant disease. Because tomato plants reproduce sexually, a male and a female plant can each contribute a set of genes. Breeding these two kinds

Farmers pick apples from a tree that was bred through hybridization, yielding bigger, juicier fruit.

of plants can create a new type of tomato plant that produces large tomatoes that are resistant to disease.

Each tomato plant has both male and female parts, however, and can self-pollinate rather than crossbreed. To be sure they crossbreed, the breeder could take away all of the male plant parts from one tomato plant, such as the one that is resistant to disease. The breeder would then take the male parts (pollen) from the other plant, the one that produces large tomatoes, and use the pollen to fertilize eggs in the female parts of the first plant. At least some of the new plants produced in this way will be hybrid tomato plants that produce large tomatoes resistant to disease.

Sometimes plant breeders pollinate by hand. They use tweezers to take pollen from the male plant part and place it on the female plant part.

BREEDING BETTER ANIMALS

Animals are also bred through selection. Cows are bred to produce more milk. Cattle and pigs are bred to produce better meat. Breeders use such techniques as artificial insemination to create these animals. They take sperm from a bull that produces a large amount of meat, for example, and use it to fertilize eggs in many cows.

There are very few animals formed by a cross between

animals of two different species. The offspring are often sterile, meaning they cannot produce offspring of their own. The best-known example of such an animal hybrid is the mule. Mules are the sterile offspring produced by crossing a female horse with a male donkey.

Since they cannot reproduce, mules are often used for labor. This is why they are often referred to as "beasts of burden."

BREEDING AND GENETIC SCIENCE

Experiments with breeding have taught scientists about genes and the rules by which genes are inherited. Genetic science developed over many years because of experiments with traditional—and slow—methods of breeding plants and animals.

Today's genetic scientists can create new plant types by inserting genes directly into cells. Inserting genes into bacteria, plants, or animals is called genetic engineering. Using enzymes that act like chemical scissors, scientists can cut out a gene from one species and insert, or splice, the gene right into a chromosome of another species. Sometimes scientists put the gene into a harmless virus, which then "infects" the plant or animal cells. The virus carries the new gene into the cell's chromosomes. Scientists can also force a gene into plant cells with a gene gun. The "gun" is a complex machine that uses high pressure to send the gene's DNA into plant cells growing in a laboratory dish.

In the 1990s, a disease was destroying the papaya crop in Hawaii. Developing a resistant fruit using traditional breeding techniques proved to be difficult. So genetic scientists used genetic engineering to develop a papaya that was resistant to the disease. They found a gene in a virus that would "vaccinate" the papaya plants against the disease. They used a gene gun to shoot the gene's DNA into the papaya cells. The geneti-

cally engineered papaya plants saved this important Hawaiian crop.

In addition to fighting disease in crop plants, scientists are learning to use genetic engineering to fight diseases in humans. They have created medicines, such as insulin, using genetic engineering techniques. They also hope to cure diseases caused by defective genes.

Papaya plants in Hawaii were saved thanks to genetic engineering.

Mendel's Peas

An Austrian monk named Gregor Mendel (1822-1884) was the first person to discover the laws of heredity. Mendel became a Catholic priest in 1847 and for the next three years studied science and mathematics at the University of Vienna. He became a high school science teacher in 1854 and lived at a monastery in what is now part of the Czech Republic.

The science of heredity came about largely because of Gregor Mendel's work.

For more than a decade, Mendel experimented in his spare time with breeding pea plants in a monastery garden. He studied seven traits in pea plants, including the flower and pod color, the height of the plant, and the shape of the seeds. He found that the traits never varied: flowers were either purple or white, and seeds were either round or wrinkled. He also found that the seven traits were passed on to the next generations in a predictable pattern. When he crossed pea plants having yellow pods with plants having green pods, all of the first-generation plants were yellow. When he bred these plants, the next generation had yellow and green pods in a ratio of 3 to 1—three pods were yellow and one was green.

Mendel came to some important conclusions. First, each trait is determined by "factors" that are passed on to descendants. An individual inherits a pair of factors for each trait, one from each of its parents. One factor is dominant, and the other factor is recessive. A trait may not show up in an individual but can still be passed on to the next generation. He also concluded that each of the seven traits was inherited independently of the others.

Mendel published his findings in 1866, but no one paid any attention. In 1900, however, scientists rediscovered Mendel's work, and the science of genetics was born. In 1909, the Danish biologist Wilhelm Ludvig Johannsen named Mendel's "factors" genes.

⊕ Genes and Disease

MEDICINE HAS CONQUERED many diseases because of scientific discoveries. In the late 1800s, Louis Pasteur discovered that infections are caused by microscopic germs. By keeping operating rooms free of germs, surgeons were able to perform lifesaving operations. In the mid-1900s, researchers discovered antibiotics that could kill bacteria that once caused deadly infections. They also developed vaccines to prevent many diseases caused by viruses, such as polio, measles, and chicken pox.

Some diseases still cannot be cured. Researchers have learned, however, that many of these diseases are caused by defects in certain genes. Genetic scientists are looking for ways to treat or cure genetic diseases.

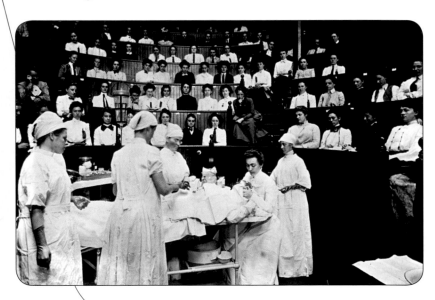

Pasteur's discoveries helped keep operating rooms sanitary, saving many lives.

GENE MUTATIONS

Original Strand

A   G   C   T   C   C   G   A

Deletion

A   G   C   T   C   C   A

Deletion: One or more nucleotides are deleted, causing the rest of the DNA code to be read differently. This may result in wrong amino acids being assembled into a protein.

Inversion

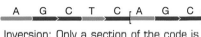

A   G   C   T   C   A   G   C

Inversion: Only a section of the code is affected, but the nucleotides are reversed in their order. In this section, inappropriate amino acids may be assembled into a protein, but the remaining DNA code is unaffected.

Substitution

A   G   C   T   C   T   G   A

Substitution: One nucleotide is replaced by another, and a different amino acid may be inserted in the protein. This type of mutation can cause diseases such as sickle cell anemia.

Insertion

A   G   C   T   C   A   C   G   A

Insertion: One or more nucleotides are inserted, and like deletion, this affects the entire DNA code. Again, wrong amino acids may be assembled into a protein.

WHEN GENES GO WRONG

When a gene is defective, the protein it codes for is also defective. Defective genes are caused by mutations. A mutation can occur when the gene is being copied during cell division. Mutations can be caused by something in the environment, such as chemicals, cigarette smoke and other pollutants, ultraviolet rays from the sun, or cosmic rays from outer space.

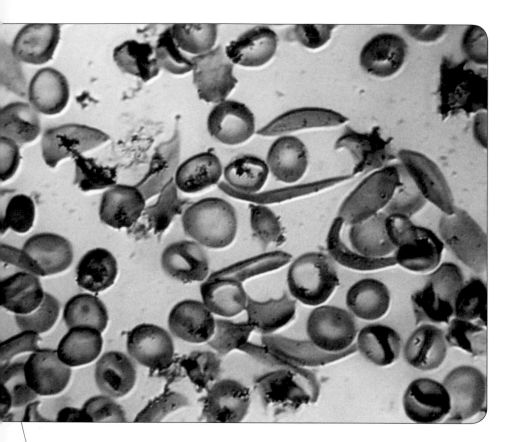

Sickle cell anemia is an inherited disease caused by a defect in the gene that codes for the protein hemoglobin. Hemoglobin in red blood cells carries oxygen in the bloodstream. Defective hemoglobin causes the red blood cells to be shaped like a sickle instead of flat and round. These sickle cells plug up small blood vessels and prevent oxygen from getting to tissues.

The odd shape of sickle cells makes it difficult for blood to travel through blood vessels.

Cancer is a disease often caused by mutations in genes that control cell division. Normally, cells only divide when they need to replace dead cells. In cancer, cells divide inappropriately and form lumps of tissue called tumors. Tumors can prevent organs from working normally. In the lungs, cancerous tumors destroy healthy tissue and prevent the lungs from taking in oxygen and giving off carbon dioxide. A cancerous tumor in the brain can destroy the centers that control many functions including speech, vision, heart rate, and breathing. Cancerous cells can also travel to other organs in the body and create new tumors that damage and destroy tissues in such organs as the liver and kidneys.

Scientists suspect that there must be mutations in several genes in order for cancer to develop. Cancer is not an inherited disease. However, some defective genes that make a person vulnerable to cancer could be inherited. Exposure to chemicals in tobacco, other pollutants, and damaging rays from the sun could cause additional mutations, leading to cancer.

DID YOU KNOW?

By 1999, scientists had cataloged more than 4,000 hereditary diseases and identified the defective proteins in several hundred of them.

TESTING GENES

Doctors can test for many of the defective genes that result in disease. The testing often begins with a blood sample. Genetic material is removed from the blood and tested for defective dominant and recessive genes. Many genetic diseases are caused by recessive genes.

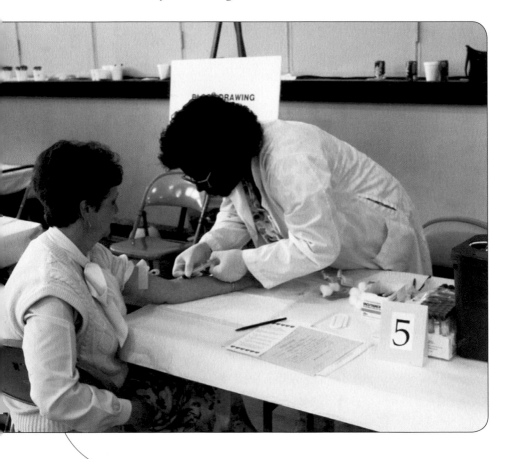

Defective genes can be identified by analyzing a person's blood.

The tests have several uses. Couples planning to have children can be tested to see whether they carry defective gene alleles. For example, cystic fibrosis causes large amounts of mucus to build up, blocking the passageway to vital organs. This results when a child inherits a recessive form of a gene from both parents.

Newborn babies can be tested to see if they have inherited genes that make them susceptible to a disease. For example, someone born with the allele of a gene that makes them susceptible to heart disease could be advised to follow a lifestyle that includes exercising regularly and eating low-fat foods.

GENETIC MEDICINE

Drug companies use genetic engineering to make some drugs. The first genetically engineered drug was human insulin for treating Type I diabetes. The bodies of people with diabetes cannot produce insulin, the hormone that removes sugar from the blood. Scientists inserted the gene for insulin into bacteria, and the bacteria became tiny drug factories that churned out vast quantities of insulin. Genetically engineered human insulin came on the market in 1982.

Researchers are working on many other medicines, including vaccines that you can eat. They are trying to insert parts of genes from disease-causing viruses into fruits and other

plants. The plant would then create a vaccine. Imagine eating applesauce that makes us immune to the flu!

Scientists want to cure genetic diseases by replacing defective genes with normal genes. In 1990, doctors used a virus to insert a normal copy of a gene into a child with a genetic disease. A faulty gene allele had crippled her body's disease-fighting immune system. The girl became well enough to attend school.

Since then, other people have been treated with gene therapy, but scientists caution that it could be many years before they know how well gene therapy works. Fortunately, scientists are constantly discovering new and exciting information on gene therapy.

Vaccines for various diseases may one day be placed in different foods, such as applesauce.

Invasion of the Alien Genes

It starts with an ache-all-over feeling and a fever. Such symptoms are common signs of influenza or the flu. The flu is caused by a virus, and these symptoms mean that the alien genes of the virus have invaded your cells. Viruses also cause other diseases, such as the common cold, measles, chicken pox, and AIDS.

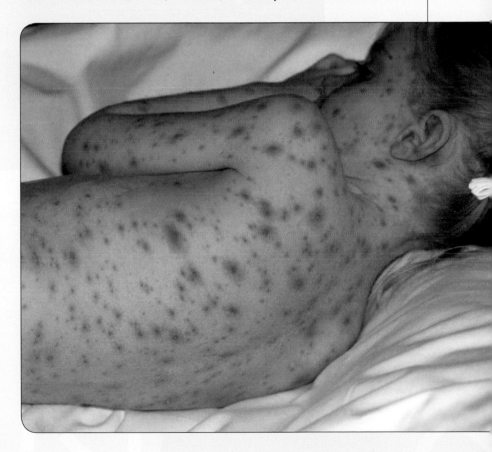

Spots, or pox, are a telltale sign of the chicken pox virus.

It is hard to say whether a virus is a living thing. A virus has genes, but the genes are not inside a cell. The genes are inside a kind of coating made of protein. A virus cannot reproduce on its own. The flu virus, for example, does not behave like a living thing until it gets into cells that line the respiratory system. Then the virus goes to work making hundreds or thousands of copies of itself.

When the flu virus invades a cell, it first sheds its outer coating. Then it dumps its genes into the cell. The viral genes take over the cell and command it to make more copies of the virus. The viral copies go on to invade other cells. The immune system goes into action to fight off the viral attack. The symptoms last until the immune system wins.

Antibiotics do not kill viruses, but vaccines can protect against many diseases caused by viruses. A vaccination containing the dead or weakened disease virus usually provides protection against the disease for many years. Flu vaccines do not work for very long, however, because the flu virus genes keep changing and mutating. Old vaccines no longer work against the mutated virus. Drug companies try to keep up with the mutations by making new flu vaccines every year.

CHAPTER FIVE

Ethics and Genetic Science

NOT EVERYONE is comfortable with many of the new developments in genetic science. Some people question the safety of genetically engineered foods and the ethics of feeding them to large numbers of people. Others have ethical concerns about the use of genetic science in medicine and how personal genetic information may be used.

ETHICS AND FOOD SAFETY

"Biological pollution" is what opponents of genetic science call genetically engineered crop plants. They point out that animal, bacterial, or viral genes could never enter plants naturally. They believe that nature should not be tampered with in this way. They also fear that mutations in any of these genes could create unknown hazards in the future.

Many people fear that genetically engineered foods might be harmful to humans. They claim that these foods have not been tested thoroughly.

Some people are concerned that pollen from plants designed to be resistant to weed killers could land on weeds. Cross-breeding with weeds, they fear, might create "superweeds" that

Many genetically engineered foods already exist in today's market.

would be difficult to kill. They also fear that plants engineered to resist insect pests could be poisonous to butterflies and other harmless insects.

Genetic scientists, however, say that there is no reason for such fears. They claim that the modified plants are safe. They point out that only one or two genes from a virus or other organism are used. They say there is no possibility of these genes causing future harm.

U.S. Food and Drug Administration (FDA) officials say that they have tested all genetically engineered crop plants. The tests show that the foods produced from these plants are safe to eat. In fact, genetically engineered foods have been part of our food supply since the late 1990s, with no known effects on humans.

Crops that have been genetically altered must be tested and monitored carefully.

Scientists are now working on genetically engineered rice, fruits, vegetables, and other crops that will be more nutritious and taste better. They must be careful, however, to be sure that these genetically engineered foods do not create allergic reactions in some people. As more genetically engineered foods become available, there are likely to be more concerns. However, the FDA must approve the safety of any new genetically engineered crops before they are allowed to enter our food supply.

ETHICS AND HUMAN GENES

Some of the most serious ethical concerns center on the uses of human genetic knowledge. It may soon be possible to know a person's complete genetic makeup. Will a new form of genetic discrimination arise?

Suppose genetic tests show that someone's genes make them more prone to heart disease. Will employers use such knowledge to deny that person a job? Will insurance companies use that knowledge to deny that person health insurance? Is it ethical to test for genetic diseases that cannot be cured? Will people who have a gene for a deadly disease such as Huntington's disease want to know?

Cloning human embryos has raised other ethical concerns. Scientists can isolate special kinds of cells called stem cells

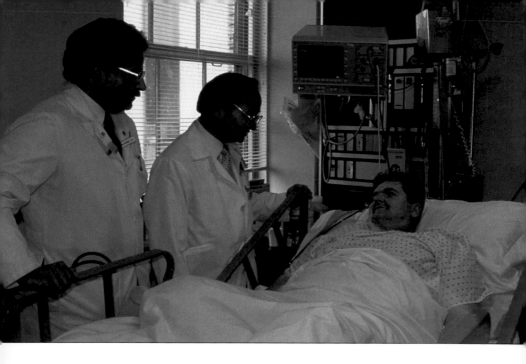

from embryos only a few days old. Research on these stem cells might lead to treatments for some incurable sicknesses, such as Parkinson's disease. Some people believe it is unethical to use human embryos for research. Other people believe it is unethical not to use such knowledge to treat sick people.

Genetic science promises great improvements in human health and wellness. It also promises to raise many questions about ethics and safety.

DID YOU KNOW?

Researchers use special regions of DNA called genetic markers to find specific genes on a chromosome. They can easily find a genetic marker. Some markers might mean a person has a defective gene and might develop a particular disease.

Stem cell research may one day yield cures to serious diseases.

Mapping Our Genes

Genetic scientists are trying to discover where every gene is on each chromosome in the human body and what each gene does. Such knowledge will help doctors diagnose genetic diseases. It will help genetic counselors give advice to couples planning to have children. It will also help researchers find cures for diseases that are caused by inborn genetic defects.

The technique for finding genes is called gene mapping. By studying inheritance patterns in a family, scientists have been able to identify the regions of chromosomes that carry certain gene alleles. Usually, the scientists were looking for gene alleles that cause a particular disease. For example, they found that the abnormal gene allele that results in Huntington's disease is on chromosome 4. Huntington's disease is a fatal disorder that kills off nerve cells in the brain. Scientists have identified more than 4,000 diseases that result from abnormal gene alleles.

Giant machines produce lasers that aid scientists in the Human Genome Project.

Mapping genes to a chromosome is somewhat like making a map of the United States that shows only the states. Scientists wanted a gene map as detailed as a map showing all the streets and every house on every block in a city. A major effort toward making such a detailed map began in 1990, with what became the Human Genome Project. Project scientists also studied the genomes of other organisms, such as bacteria and mice. By 2003, this international project had sequenced and analyzed the nucleotide base order of DNA in the entire human genome. The scientists had mapped almost 20,000 human genes. They believe that the human genome may contain about 25,000 genes.

The Human Genome Project scientists have put their findings into a huge computer databank. Other researchers all over the world can study this information to learn what each gene does and what can happen should it become abnormal. All of this information has the potential to be put to use to improve human health. Many leaders concerned about ethical issues, however, want to be sure that it cannot be used to do harm.

alleles—alternate forms of the same gene

blueprint—diagram that shows how to construct a building or other project

chromosomes—threadlike structures in the nucleus that carry the genes

clones—organisms with the exact same genes as the organisms that produced them

crossing over—switching genes from one chromosome to another

DNA (deoxyribonucleic acid)—the chemical of which genes are made

dominant allele—the allele form of a gene most likely to produce a trait in offspring

ethics—concerns about what is morally right or wrong

genes—the basic units of heredity

genetic engineering—inserting genes from one organism into the chromosomes of another organism

genome—complete set of genes in an organism

genotype—combination of gene alleles in an organism

hybrid—cross between different male and female plants or animals to produce offspring with desired traits

mutation—a change resulting in a new biological trait or characteristic

nucleus—the command center of the cell that gives instructions to the other parts of the cell

phenotype—traits expressed by genes in an organism

Punnett square—device for figuring the probability of which alleles will be expressed to give an individual traits

recessive allele—gene most likely to stay "hidden"

somatic cell—body cell; any cell except a sex cell

vaccinate—exposing the immune system to a dead or weakened form of a virus or germ so the body can fight off an infection

zygote—an egg that has been fertilized by a sperm

▸ Many genetic experiments have been carried out on a species of fruit fly called *Drosophila melanogaster.* It is only about 0.12 inch (3 millimeters) long, so scientists can easily keep large numbers of these flies in laboratories. This fly has only eight chromosomes, so its genes and traits are easy to study. Also, it produces new generations rapidly because its life span is only about two weeks.

▸ Hemophilia, a disorder in which blood cannot clot properly, usually affects only boys. The defective gene for a protein that helps blood clot is on the X chromosome. Boys have only one X chromosome. Girls have two X chromosomes, and at least one usually has a normal blood-clotting gene. In rare cases, girls can inherit hemophilia if the genes on both X chromosomes are defective. If she has one defective gene and one normal gene, she can pass the disorder on to a son. Genes on X or Y chromosomes are called sex-linked genes.

▸ World leaders in the 1960s feared that poor people in Mexico and Asia might not be able to grow enough food. To prevent mass starvation, scientists bred new varieties of wheat and rice. The new crop plants yielded more grain and gave people plenty of food. The work of the scientists was called the Green Revolution.

▸ Luther Burbank (1849-1926) was one of the most famous plant breeders in America. He crossed many kinds of plants and produced new kinds of plums, potatoes, and other food plants. The most common potato grown today, the Russett Burbank, comes from his work.

▸ American geneticist Barbara McClintock made many important discoveries about genes by studying corn. In 1931, she explained that crossing over results when genes trade places on chromosomes during meiosis. In the 1950s, she discovered "jumping genes," also called transposons or "mobile genetic elements." These genes can move from one place to another on a chromosome and affect other genes. She won the 1983 Nobel Prize for Medicine.

Luther Burbank, developer of more than 800 strains of plants, tends to his garden.

Christian Academy
of Prescott
Library

At the Library

Day, Trevor. *Genetics*. San Diego: Blackbirch Press, 2004.
George, Linda. *Gene Therapy*. San Diego: Blackbirch Press, 2003.
Glimm, Adele. *Gene Hunter: The Story of Neuropsychologist Nancy Wexler*. New York: Franklin Watts, 2005.
Walker, Richard. *Genes and DNA*. Boston: Kingfisher, 2003.

On the Web

For more information on **genetics,** use FactHound to track down Web sites related to this book.
1. Go to *www.facthound.com*
2. Type in a search word related to this book or this book ID: **0756516188**
3. Click on the *Fetch It* button.
FactHound will find the best Web sites for you.

On the Road

The Genomic Revolution
American Museum of Natural History
Central Park West at 79th Street
New York, NY 10024-5192
212/313-7278

Genetics: Decoding Life
Museum of Science and Industry
5700 S. Lake Shore Drive
Chicago, IL 60637-2093 USA
773/684-1414

Explore all the books in this series:

Animal Cells: Smallest Units of Life
ISBN: 0-7565-1616-1

Chemical Change: From Fireworks to Rust
ISBN: 0-7565-1256-5

DNA: The Master Molecule of Life
ISBN: 0-7565-1617-X

Erosion: How Land Forms, How It Changes
ISBN: 0-7565-0854-1

Genetics: A Living Blueprint
ISBN: 0-7565-1618-8

Manipulating Light: Reflection, Refraction, and Absorption
ISBN: 0-7565-1258-1

Minerals: From Apatite to Zinc
ISBN: 0-7565-0855-X

Natural Resources: Using and Protecting Earth's Supplies
ISBN: 0-7565-0856-8

Physical Change: Reshaping Matter
ISBN: 0-7565-1257-3

Plant Cells: The Building Blocks of Plants
ISBN: 0-7565-1619-6

Soil: Digging Into Earth's Vital Resources
ISBN: 0-7565-0857-6

Waves: Energy on the Move
ISBN: 0-7565-1259-X